The Big Pond

By Nell Grafton

Edited by Matt Mosler

xulon PRESS

Copyright © 2006 by Nell Grafton

The Big Pond
by Nell Grafton

Printed in the United States of America

ISBN 1-59781-881-X

All rights reserved solely by the author. The author guarantees all contents are original and do not infringe upon the legal rights of any other person or work. No part of this book may be reproduced in any form without the permission of the author. The views expressed in this book are not necessarily those of the publisher.

Unless otherwise indicated, Bible quotations are taken from the New American Standard Bible. Copyright © 1960, 1962, 1963, 1968, 1971, 1972, 1973, 1975, 1977 by The Lockman Foundation.

www.xulonpress.com

Foreword

Nell Grafton has the gift of evangelism and allows the Lord to use her to tell people the good news of Salvation.

I have known Nell for many years and had the privilege of seeing her trained in personal evangelism. From the start it was obvious that the Lord had anointed her with a great gift. She was bold and unafraid to tell others about Jesus in any circumstance. When Nell would go out for the purpose of sharing her faith her only fear was that people would not accept Christ.

One of the most vivid memories of mine is the time Nell saw a man on the other side of a parking lot alone at night and she said, *"That man needs to know about Jesus."* She ran over to him and excitedly began to tell him about her personal and precious Savior, Christ Jesus.

Nell is an inspiration to others to be faithful in witnessing in season and out of season.

—James Weedman

It is my prayer, that as you read this book, you will enjoy the adventures Nell has had in sharing her faith, and you will also have a desire to share your faith with others.

I always look forward to hearing her latest adventure with God. I have known Nell for many years and have enjoyed being her friend. I remember one night we had a bunking party, just to hear Nell share her stories. Believe it or not, she talked all night long. There will be many people in heaven because of her faithfulness and obedience to God.

She has been blessed with a wonderful gift and in turn has been a blessing to many.

—Anne Weedman

Jim and Ann Weedman are SBC Missionaries to Guatemala.

A number of years ago, I took a study course entitled Evangelism Explosion or E.E. There were a number of people in the class, including Dr. Jim Weedman and Nell Grafton. As the class progressed we went out three by three to witness. Two of us would pray while the other witnessed.

This continued for several weeks and then months; however, with Nell, it has continued for years. This lifestyle continues today and eternity alone will reveal the number of saints who are in Heaven because of the witness of Nell Grafton. Only then will the whole story of Nell Grafton and her witness be revealed.

I praise God for the life of this special woman.

Bob Mayhan
Deacon, Immanuel Baptist Church
El Dorado, Arkansas

The Big Pond

Brother James and his wife Nell Grafton are two very special people.

Every one who knows Nell knows she loves to fish for both men and fish and we look forward to hearing about someone else she has led to the Lord.

Our prayer is that this book will help someone else to want to witness also.

Pastor Chris Morgan
Eagle Mills Baptist Church
Camden, Arkansas

Nell Grafton is the most excited and the most consistent soul winner I have ever known!

The welfare of every soul is her concern. I have never seen anything turn her back from pursuing her mission of helping everyone to come to know Jesus. She is a real inspiration to all who know her.

Pastor Don Moore
Former President,
Arkansas Baptist State Convention

Introduction

I will never forget the first time I met Nell Grafton. She was telling a fish story. Really.

I had just finished speaking at a church in the local Baptist association where her husband James was the director of missions. After the service the pastor of the church and his family, my family along with Nell and James all went back to the fellowship hall to eat a meal prepared by some of the ladies in the church. This is good, southern hospitality at it's finest! I was seated next to Nell. When someone is feeding you it's always best to play nice so I started up a trivial conversation just to be pleasant. That's when she began to regale me with one of the most fantastic fish stories I've ever heard.

It seemed there was this pond near her house. She called it "the Big Pond." Whenever she had a free moment, she said, she would grab her rod and reel, her tackle box and a chair and head on down to the Big Pond. This one particular day things had been going slowly. She hadn't had too much action on her lure so she prayed. As you'll find out later in this book…God answers Nell's prayers. Nell prayed that if God would give her a big fish she would share the gospel with the next person who came to the big pond. It was about that time that her rod nearly bent in two.

The Big Pond

I chuckled as this sweet southern lady recalled the story of how God had answered her prayer so quickly by putting a huge fish on her line. She said she struggled to reel in what she guessed was at least a 5 pound bass. As she got close to pulling that big guy ashore he broke the line and swam away. Nell was so mad. Not only had she lost that big fish but he took one of her favorite lures as well. Somewhat defeated Nell went home shortly after that but she couldn't get that fish off of her mind.

Later that same day she told her husband, James, that she was going back to the Big Pond to catch that fish and get her lure back. James, as he's learned to do over the years, just smiled and let her go knowing somewhere deep down that sure as the sun rises Nell was going to catch that fish and get her lure back.

When she returned to the pond she again said a prayer asking for God to help her catch that fish. On her first cast, she said, her lure wasn't in the water but a few seconds when "wham" her rod again bent nearly in two. With all her strength and skill Nell fought that fish all the way to the shore but this time she landed him. When she pulled him out of the water…you guessed it…her favorite lure was still hooked to his lip.

Nell was so excited she couldn't wait to get home and tell James. James marveled at the size of the fish and patiently listened to his wife tell of God's goodness. Then, feeling that this fish was indeed a gift straight from the hand of God James and Nell decided tonight was the night for fried fish. As James prepared to filet the big bass he was surprised to find another lure; a beautiful, shiny, green lure that looked to be nearly brand new inside the belly of the fish. What a blessing, Nell thought! Not only had God helped retrieve her favorite lure but he'd given her another one to boot!

Thinking that was the end of the story I laughed and tried to get back to my poppy seed chicken casserole but

Nell wasn't finished. "That's not the whole story," she said. "Listen to this!"

It seemed that Nell was so excited with her prior days catch that she returned to the Big Pond early the next day. Again she tied on her favorite lure and began the quest for another lunker. It wasn't long before a fishing boat trolled on by. Always looking for opportunities to share the gospel Nell began to tell the men about the big fish that she caught the day before. One of the men on the boat said he, too, had hooked a fish yesterday that sounded about that big. But just like Nell's that fish got away with his favorite lure. He didn't know where on earth he was going to find another shiny, green lure like that one again. That's when Nell reached down into her tackle box and asked, "Did it look anything like this one?"

The man couldn't believe his eyes as God, using Nell as his vessel, returned to that man his lure as well. Nell then used the opportunity to share the gospel with the two men on that boat and won them both to the Lord!

That story, which Nell swears to me is true, was just one of many she told me about the opportunities God has given her to share the gospel not just on the Big Pond but everywhere this lady goes. Nell Grafton is a witnessing dynamo. She witnesses to people she knows. She witnesses to people she doesn't know. She witnesses to white people, black people, men, women, young people and old codgers. She's witnessed to artists and cowboys. She's even won telemarketers to the Lord! But as you'll see in this book Nell isn't any different than you or me. She's just so on fire for her Lord that she's always looking for ways to turn the conversation toward Jesus.

Nell is a wonderful storyteller and I know these stories will entertain and inspire you so enjoy them. But there are also a few things I want you to notice about Nell's ministry.

First, notice that before Nell ever says a word to anyone she prays. Jesus said, "You didn't choose me but I chose you." (Jn. 15:16) Nell firmly believes that God will lead you to the person to whom you are to be a witness.

Next, notice her preparation. Nell knows her scriptures. She knows them well enough to present a clear message. She doesn't win people with her philosophy but backs up her claims with chapter and verse.

Third, Nell's message is relevant to her listener. The gospel transcends race and gender and its message is never compromised. Though it may not appear so on the surface Nell always finds common ground with the people with whom she shares.

Fourth, I'm astounded at the courage of this lady. God often led Nell into situations many of us would never go. She is not a super hero. She does not possess superhuman skill. She only possesses a faith in her father to protect her while she enters the battlefield. She is willing to deny herself, take up her cross and follow him.

Next, notice that regardless of where she is or what she's doing Nell is always ready and available. When God called she responded. Oftentimes, you'll notice, she prayed that God would use her that day and was always ready when she felt him call.

Sixth, more than courageous you should be encouraged by Nell's boldness. Jesus told the frightened disciples in the boat, *"Be Bold, I AM, Fear Not."* Matt. 14:27 (paraphrase) Nell knows Jesus is who he says he is. She also knows that unless she shares the good news with his children they will die and go to Hell. That confidence and that urgency allow her to seek out opportunities to share. She goes where others would be intimidated to go in order to share the gospel because that's her job.

Finally, sense the humility of this godly woman. Nell does not take any credit whatsoever for these decisions. Time

The Big Pond

and time again you will read that it was God who saved these people. Nell was just the vehicle he chose. (I Cor. 3:6)

Now, I don't want to paint Nell into a corner as a "super Christian." She's a wife, a mother, a grandmother, a fisherman, a storyteller and a heckuva nice lady among other things. Jesus said he came that we may *"have life and might have it abundantly."* (Jn. 10:10) Nell is a lady who lives her life to the full but is always mindful that the mission of her life, and yours as well, is to *"proclaim the excellencies of him who has called you out of darkness and into his marvelous light."* (I Peter 2:9) How you 'proclaim his excellencies' is between you and God.

On a quick technical note, some of you may be wondering why I organized the stories the way I did. Honestly that was a major quandary. Should they be in chronological order? Should they be organized according to subject? Or should I leave them just as Nell recorded them? I opted for the latter for the simple reason that Nell, in the grand southern tradition, is a delightful story teller and reading the stories in this manner is the closest you, the reader, can get to actually having lunch with Nell Grafton.

It's my prayer that these stories will inspire you to share God's word with others, encourage you to follow him wherever he leads and motivate you to fulfill your ministry just as Nell is fulfilling hers.

Fight on!

Matt Mosler
Beautiful Feet Ministries

-1-

Squealing Brakes

We retired from Corning, AR and bought a home in Thornton, AR, where James had pastored First Baptist Church in 1992 and 1993. We had unpacked all of our boxes and put them out at the curb to be picked up. The unpacking exhausted us! I walked out to the front porch and sat in the swing.

I began to pray, "God, what could I do for you today?" Suddenly, I heard brakes squealing, I knew a truck was coming around the bend of the big pond.

Now, the big pond is 21-acres and just through the tiny wood thicket from our house. It takes me about five minutes to get there. This is where I have witnessed to many, many people as I sat on the bank fishing. This is where you have a common denominator, people that love to fish and be in an outdoor world.

I said, "God, I hear those brakes; I will be your witness." Quickly, I went in the house, got two *New Testaments,* and met the men at the road.

As I started to shake hands with the first one, he began to smile from ear to ear and said, "Remember me?"

"No, where have I met you before?" I answered.

"You led me to Jesus six years ago over on the big pond levee where we rejoiced! You need to talk to my partner." Then I turned to the driver and shared the gospel with a lost man. God saved him.

"Well, he is not my regular helper, "the driver said, "my regular helper is out for the day."

"Maybe I can talk to him when he returns to work."

The next morning I had shampooed my hair, rolled it up on brush curlers, and put on my old slacks. I was going to clean house for the day.

Suddenly, James called from the back porch, "Nell!"

"What?" I replied.

"A man is out here that would like to see you."

Like this, I thought? Nevertheless, God does not care. He just looks at your heart. I walked out on the porch.

There stood a man saturated with red mud from head to toe. He ran to me saying, "I want you to tell me how to be saved!"

We shared the gospel with him, in a circle, holding hands and praying as he asked the Lord, Jesus Christ to come into his life.

It was such a joy! God has given me an opportunity to witness to every one of those city workers. They are all going into God's Kingdom today.

-2-

Fishers of Men

James and I had planned to go to Heber Springs, Arkansas for three days and about 4:00 on the evening before we were to leave, I told him I was going over to the big pond to fish for a while. He said, "Nell, don't you bring a fish to this house. I have four acres to mow before dark."

Well, I went to the big pond and there were several people on the levee fishing, so I sat down on the bank, cast one time and caught a 3-pound bass. There was a man standing to my left about thirty yards and I held him up and said, "Would you like to have this bass?" He said, "I surely would."

So I said, "Come put him on your stringer, and if I catch anymore, I'll give them to you."

Well, God really put me to a test when I uttered those words. They just rolled out of me. So, I sat back down, made one more cast and caught a 5-pound bass. In my heart, I was going to keep this one to put in our own pond. I looked, and this man was running back toward me because he saw me catch that fish. When he got to me, he said, "Are you gonna keep that bass, or are you gonna give him to me?"

Well, it just automatically came out, "I'm gonna give him to you. Put your thumb in his lower jaw so you can take the hook out of his mouth." And the Lord just prompted my spirit. This was such an exciting event why not take this opportunity to share the gospel with this man?

As he was holding his thumb in the lower jaw of that 5-pound bass, I said, "I want to share something with you. I'm gonna give you this fish, and it's a joy to share him with you, but I want to know where you are spiritually." This man, a 65-year-old deacon in the church, did not know for sure that he would go to Heaven, but he does now.

Praise the mighty name of Jesus Christ!

-3-

Fit to Use

This is the story about an African-American that I met in Homer, Louisiana back in 1984. We were at the lake for the summer and one morning I got up to take the laundry to town and I began to pray that God would use me to be his witness all day long. I remembered a little farmhouse back in the woods on a gravel road and I knew this man raised purple hull peas. So my objective was to go to his house first and get some peas, then go into town to the Laundromat. I found his house. He was not at home, but his 9-year-old son was sitting on some old broken concrete steps in front of the house. I sat down beside him and shared the Lord Jesus Christ and the plan of salvation. Holding to my hands, he prayed and asked the Lord to come into his life and give him that gift of eternal life. And I said, "Thank you, Lord. I praise you for this. Just use me again. I'm willing."

I got to town and I picked up the mail before I left the house. For people that owned property on Lake Claiborne, there was a rural newspaper publication that was sent out monthly. I got this newspaper, went to the Laundromat, put my clothes in the washer and sat down to read the paper. There was a full-page article about an African-American man named David Allen who had been interviewed. His picture was in the paper and his first words were, "God's got it fixed where everybody can do something special. Just to live and die ain't all that much. Leave a mark. Be your best at whatever you want to do and you'll be remembered by it."

The story went on to talk about how he was one of two walking-stick carvers in the state of Louisiana. President Reagan had flown him and his wife to Washington, D.C. where he had presented one of his walking sticks to President Reagan. There was one in the Smithsonian Institute and several in the museums of Louisiana. He went on to share that his carving designs must have just been passed down to him unknowingly from his African ancestors. As I read his article, he was telling the story of how, when he was a young boy, he found a knife and he knew his parents wouldn't let him keep it, so he hid it from his family because they wouldn't let a kid that young have a knife.

Well, he hid it under the house on one of the posts. When he would go walking, he would take that knife with him. He would spot a sapling and he pulled it up and in the root system he could visualize carving a deer, a bird, a butterfly, or a fish, something of nature that God had created.

As years went by he said he was walking into Homer, Louisiana one summer day and got real hot. He sat down under a tree and noticed a sapling. He cut it off and began to carve into the bark an intricate design. He carved on it for two weeks. When the bark dried, it popped off. He said, "You know, that's the way God is. He has to take the rough outer shell of our lives and remove that so that he can get down to the part that's pliable where he can use us." This was an awesome testimony to me. As I read this article, I began to pray and I said, "Lord, I want to meet this man. I know he is a man of God."

I looked out the window of the Laundromat, and across the street was a hamburger stand and out at the picnic tables were two ladies. I walked over and showed the paper to them and asked if they knew this man. They said, "Yes, that's David Allen." They didn't know that he and his wife had flown to Washington, D.C. to present one of his walking sticks to President Reagan, or that one was in the Smithsonian Institute and several were in museums all over the state of Louisiana.

I began to pray that God would use me in this witness opportunity. They said, "Well, why don't we get in your car and we'll take you to his home?" So we got to his home where two men were sitting in cane-bottom chairs out under a shade tree in the front yard. Two men were cutting each of their friend's hair. I asked if David Allen was home. Over in the corner of the yard was a 29-year-old man shelling a bushel of purple hull peas. David's wife came out on the porch and I told her who I was and why I had come. She said, "Anytime anyone wants to talk about the Lord in my yard, they are welcome."

Well, God prompted my spirit and I began to pray, "What better opportunity, Lord, than to share the gospel with these people." There were two out in my car, four nearby, and one shelling peas. I questioned all of them one-on-one, asked their names and ages, and the first diagnostic question that we had been trained to ask, "Have you come to the point in your spiritual life that you know for certain that if you were to die today that you'd go to Heaven?" Every response was, "No, I know I would go to Hell."

Well, I shared the gospel with them and in a circle in that front yard, every one of them prayed to receive the Lord. I made an appointment to come back the next day to meet David Allen. When we got back in the car, and reached the Laundromat, another lady who was a friend of theirs walked up. She had folded all my clothes and had them in a basket.

I said, "Well, y'all have been so good to me, what can I do for you? Could I carry you home?" because they were all walking. They said no because they had to stop by Wal-Mart and I said, "That's on my way. I'll carry you to Wal-Mart." Well, when we got to Wal-Mart, I realized there was one in the car I had not witnessed to and I shared the gospel with her. She was lost and she asked Jesus Christ to come into her heart and life. This was a special day for me.

The next day, I went to see David Allen and he and his wife invited me in. I gave him one of my paintings of a butterfly. It was a glass painting done in pearl and gold. He was so proud. I listened to his testimony and he was sharing about that bark coming off. I mentioned that to him. He said, "Yes, that's the way God has to get our attention to make the best of our lives." And I'll never forget the three words he used. I wrote these three words down in my Bible – to make us "fit to use," vessels for him, fit to use. I still cherish the hand-carved walking stick he gave to me.

I've told this story numerous times in the last twenty years and it gets more precious every day. I thank God that He gives me the opportunity just to simply tell others how much He loves them. This was May, 1984 so this week as I begin this writing twenty years later, this is June and as I began to think about writing this story, I began to think, "Well, his phone number is at the bottom of this article. I'll just call him and see how he and his family are doing." So, I called and he answered the phone. I said, "David, this is Nell Grafton. Do you remember my coming to your home and giving you a pearl and gold butterfly?" He said, "I'm sitting here looking at it."

I did not know until I went back to meet him that day that two of those men I led to the Lord were his sons. I said, "I want to know how your sons that prayed to receive the Lord are doing.

The Big Pond

"One of them is living for the Lord, happy as can be, the other one is a preacher who pastors two churches today," he said.

You see God is so good. It's just wonderful just to talk about His precious name.

-4-

"God Sent You Here!"

My mother and dad lived in Dubach, Louisiana and it was a 20-mile trip from our lake place to their home. I got up one morning and I began to pray, *"God, I'm going to see Mama and Daddy today and I pray that this will be a mission for you."* In my heart I knew every house on that road and I knew that African-American people lived in most of those homes.

As I was getting ready to leave, I began to pray that God would show me what to do. In my mind's eye, God implanted one particular witness in my spiritual vision and it happened at the end of the day exactly like he showed me.

At the first house I stopped, I drove up in the yard and the yard had been swept clean and it was nothing but red, clay, hard, dirt. But there was a maze through the most beautiful flowerbed that I have ever seen. I have seen these flowers blooming every summer in many yards, but I got my book out and looked up the name of this particular flower. They were called cleome and these plants were six-feet tall, just a beautiful sight.

I walked up to the door and knocked on the door and this elderly African-American lady opened the door. I told her who I was and that I had something I'd like to share with her and she invited me in. I asked her if she was there alone and she said, her husband was in the back yard. I asked her if she would get him to come in?

She called him and he came in. As we were sitting there in the living room, it was a beautiful bright sunny day. I shared the gospel with both of them. Both of them had no knowledge that they would go to heaven, and they both wanted to be saved. When we got on our knees in a circle to pray, lightning struck that house and knocked the electricity out. It didn't startle any of us. She got up from her knees and she said, *"Just a minute."* She walked over and she flipped off that light switch. (You know, Satan makes his appearance but we have to recognize this.) Then they prayed to receive the Lord into their lives. We hugged each other and they kept saying, *"Thank you for stopping at our house. God sent you here."*

I left that house and went across the road and shared the gospel where two other people there prayed to receive the Lord. I went on around the bend and stopped at another house. This elderly couple was sitting out on their porch in rocking chairs, shelling peas. When I walked up, I told them who I was and that I had something I'd like to share with them. When I began to talk about the Lord, they got so excited and started rocking just as fast as they could rock. As I was telling them how they could be saved, they were saying, *"Glory, hallelujah! Hallelujah, God sent you here!"* And both of those, a man and his wife, prayed to receive the Lord!

-5-

Family Affair

*N*ow over the years, most every time we went from Homer to Dubach, there was a man walking with a cane and I knew about where he would be. I began to pray, and I said, *"Lord, if he's out walking today, I know that it is your will for me to stop and witness to him."* And when I made that bend, there he was walking toward me on the shoulder of the road.

I pulled my van off and got out, and asked him if I could share something with him. Well, he invited me to his house. I said, *"Well, where do you live? Is your wife at home?"* He said that she was and showed me where he lived. It was back off the hill on the side of the road. We walked up to his house, and God had this all planned from the beginning. When we went in to his living room, there were thirteen members of his family in the living room!

I sat down on the sofa and I questioned all of them, got their ages and names, and every one of them said that they had no idea that they'd go to heaven and they wanted to know how they could be saved. In a circle in that living room I shared the gospel with them, including the elderly man with the cane and his wife, and asked them to repeat the sinner's prayer after me. I made them to understand that they weren't praying to me, that this was between them and God, and that God's promise was that He would have the angels write their names down in the Lamb's Book of Life. And that God went on to say something more special. He said, *"I'll engrave your name on the palms of my hands." Is. 49:16 (paraphrase)* Nobody loves us that much, only God Himself.

As they began to pray, the child sitting to my left holding my hand prayed out loud above every voice in that circle. I did not acknowledge this child or address him when I was sharing the gospel. But he had heard every word that I shared and he prayed, *"Dear God, have mercy on me, a sinner. Come into my heart and save me from my sins. Thank you God, for giving me this gift of eternal life. I want to live for you and be your witness. In the name of Jesus Christ, I pray, Amen."*

When we finished praying, I looked over at this child and I said, *"Son, how old are you?"* And he held up six fingers. Praise God! The Lord built him a mansion that day in heaven. This has been twenty years ago. I pray God called him into the ministry.

On around the curve, I remembered a house that always had a brown car under the carport. And I prayed, *"Lord, if that car is there I will stop."* And when I got to the house, that brown car was sitting under the carport. I got out, knocked on the door, and this lady came to the door and said, *"God sent you here. I've been so depressed I needed someone to talk to."*

God saved her that morning and gave her the gift of eternal life

-6-

Grave Digger

As I was working on this book, we were called and told that one of my dearest friends of thirty years had passed away in El Dorado. I know that she was a Christian and I know she's in Heaven. God led me to do an awesome thing at the cemetery while the family and friends were gathered there at the graveside as we talked about our precious friend. The pastor took my friends Bible and through the things she had written in the margins allowed her to preach her own sermon. The sayings, the stories and her personal life were recorded in God's precious word.

As we started back toward the van after the graveside service and James got in I looked out and saw an African-American man walking across the gravesites drinking a coke. I didn't even stop at the van because God told me to keep walking. I walked out to him, shook his hand and said, "Did you help dig the grave?"

"Yes, ma'am, I did," he said.

"Well, I'm a Southern Baptist preacher's wife. I'd just like to visit with you and ask you a question. Have you come to the point in your spiritual life that you know for sure if you were to die today that you'd go the Heaven?"

"Well, I've done the best I can," he said.

"Well, Ephesians (2:8 KJV) says, 'For by grace (that's God's grace) are you saved through faith; and that not of yourselves: it is the gift of God' for those that believe." I shared the gospel with him and he put that coke on the ground, took my hands and prayed to receive the Lord into his life.

He was 65 years old. You see we don't assume that everybody has the peace, joy and assurance of salvation. We have to ask because we care, because someone cared enough to share with us. Thank you, Lord.

-7-

Heart to Heart

Back in 1981 my older brother, Clyde, was taken to Baptist Hospital in Little Rock to have heart surgery. He needed five heart bypasses. Our family went up to be with him and all of the family was praying for him. So, when they took him into surgery I just quietly slipped away from the family and went down to the chapel to pray for Clyde.

When I walked into the chapel, there was an African-American lady about 29 years old sitting on the 2nd row. She was the only person in the chapel. She had her head down and was crying. So, I just walked down, sat down beside her, put my arm around her and said, "Can we talk about it?"

She just leaned over on my shoulder and cried her heart out. She said, "My husband has just been taken into surgery to have a double bypass." They were both from El Dorado. We prayed for my brother and her husband. Then I witnessed to her, and she said, "No, I don't know for certain I'm going to Heaven."

"Well, do you want to know for sure that when you die that you will go to Heaven?" I asked.

"Yes, I do," she answered. So I shared the gospel with her. She took my hands and prayed to receive the Lord into her life. We were both crying then we were both praising the Lord together.

"When I get my husband home, would you come to my house and tell my husband what you just told me?" she asked. "He's not saved." I said I would come and she gave me directions.

A few weeks later, God reminded me that I had not followed through with that promise. So I began to pray, "God, I'm not sure where this address is, but I pray that you'll lead and guide me." So I drove to El Dorado, turned at the old Coca-Cola Bottling plant and began to weave my way into that area. I got out of the car and asked two different people for directions. They were skeptical of my being there, and it just seemed like they were leading me on a wild goose chase with the directions they gave me.

In a few minutes, I was standing in a chicken yard and fear came across me from head to toe. It was as though Satan said, "You're in a strange neighborhood. You don't know where you're really standing. You could be in danger." My heart just sank to my feet and immediately the spirit of the Lord came upon me and said, "Follow Me."

I looked toward Heaven and said, "God, I was invited here. I pray that you will just lead and I will follow you." I turned around, and to my back was the back porch of a little shanty house. The woman from the chapel was standing in the door. She had already seen me and called for me to come.

I went over there and followed her into the room where her husband was still in bed. It was a little shanty, but it was immaculate, clean as a pin. She pulled up a chair beside his bed, and I shared the gospel with a man that just wanted to know how he could be saved. He, his wife and I held hands in a circle as he prayed and asked Jesus Christ to come into his life, to forgive his sins and become his savior. We hugged and I told them I would be praying for them.

As I turned around to go out the door, I didn't know that his older sister was standing in the doorway to the kitchen. She had heard everything I had said to her brother and was standing there with tears in her eyes. She said, "What about me?" I turned and shared the gospel with her and she prayed to receive the Lord into her life as well.

Thank you, Lord for being so good and faithful to us when we trust in you.

-8-

Look For Me

I had just learned the song "Look For Me" by Rusty Goodman. He was very much ahead of his day in writing gospel music. He's in Heaven today but his songs are still special and still have messages for the world to hear.

The phone rang about 10:00 in the morning as I was cooking lunch, and this telemarketer named Don began to ask me about a magazine that I had a subscription to. I said, "I don't want to renew it at this time," and God just prompted my spirit to witness to him.

Now, I understand that those telemarketers have about 3 minutes and I said, "Don, I'm Nell Grafton. Where are you calling from?"

"Ohio," he said. I asked if I could talk to him for a minute and he talked to me like he had forty days and forty nights to listen.

I began to witness to him and he broke down and cried and cried and cried. He said, "My wife has left me. My divorce is final today and I've lost my children and my home. I don't have anything to live for."

I said, "Could I share something wonderful with you?" and I shared the gospel with him. He prayed to receive the Lord over the phone. I said, "I want you to know that there's a little lady in Thornton, Arkansas on her knees praying for you everyday, and I pray God's very best for you. You do have something to live for."

I went on to share with him that I had just been singing the song "Look For Me" when the phone rang. "I want you to know, Don," I said. "When we get to Heaven, you look for me because I'm going to be there, too, looking for you."

After I hung up, I realized that this man was on the brink of suicide. He had given up.

He had no hope. But now in Jesus Christ, he has hope.

-9-

I Thirst!

I have three sisters and two brothers. One day while we were living in Corning, Arkansas (James was the Director of Missions for the local association) one of my sisters called me and told me that they had put her husband Bill, who was my age, into the hospital in Ruston, Louisiana. He had a leaking aneurysm and no doctor in Louisiana would touch him. They said it would be fatal if they did surgery. A friend of theirs had an airplane and he volunteered to fly Bill to the hospital in Houston where the doctors said that they would treat him. All of our family and friends were much in prayer for Bill. I drove the 8-hour drive from Corning to Ruston, met my other two sisters and we drove eight more hours down into Houston.

At 2:00 a.m. we went into ICU and we prayed Bill to the throne of grace, asking God to heal him. Along with the prayers of many friends and all our family, we felt that

God was working in his life. God did a miracle for him. He healed him.

I made the 8-hour drive back to El Dorado, Arkansas, spent the night with our daughter and her family, got up the next morning and I was going to drive on to Corning. I was by myself and I had just learned the song that Bev Lowery wrote entitled "I Thirst." I began to pray, *"God, what can I do for you these next hours?"*

I heard him in my spirit say, *"Sing, Nell, Sing."* I started singing "I thirst." When I got to Calion, Arkansas, to my left I saw a neon sign that read "Liquor" over a store. Three men sat out on the rail by that store. I kept going and the Lord spoke to me and said, *"You asked what you could do for me today. Those men thirst but they thirst for the wrong thing. Go back, Nell, and tell them about the living water that I can give them and they'll never thirst again."*

And Satan said so quickly, *"You don't have a place to turn around before you go across that Ouachita River Bridge."* God blocked that out. There was a driveway that I could turn around in and I pulled off, turned around and drove up into that driveway where those men were sitting.

I told them who I was and all three of them were lost without Jesus Christ. The man sitting in the middle of the rail was named Willie. The fourth man walked up in the midst of this witness and I included him. He was also lost. All of them prayed to receive the Lord holding hands in a circle there in front of that liquor store at 10:00 that morning.

Satan made his appearance by the traffic. We were standing about twenty yards from Highway 167 and when they began to pray holding hands in a circle, I know there had to be thirty 18-wheeler trucks that rushed by taking the very voice from me. But I waited until they passed and I finished this witness and their prayer. I told them that I was singing "I Thirst" when I passed them by, and I was going to sing it to them. It didn't matter to me what the world thought.

I stood there and I sang that song a cappella, praising the Lord Jesus Christ for what he had just done. Thank you Jesus for this opportunity to share God's word!

-10-

Dungeons & Dragons

When we went back to Texas, James was in Seminary. First Baptist Church in Waxahachie appointed us to do mission work in a mobile home park there in Waxahachie where there were 1200 people. I had taken classes to learn how to reverse glass paint and I had painted numerous pictures and had them framed. I probably had 25 or 30 that were size 16 x 20 and 24 x 36. Someone invited me to be a part of an art show that they were having in Waxahachie at the new Boy Scout building.

The day I got to the building, the director asked me where I wanted to set up my paintings. I said, *"Well, this is up to you. You show me."* There were two adjoining buildings and she steered me to the entrance of the gymnasium and told me to set up there. Well, I did and I had prayed, *"God, show me what you want me to do for you today. Just use me and teach me how to be a witness."*

The Big Pond

A 19-year-old Spanish boy came by my booth numerous times and he would speak every time he came by. I said, *"Lord, what are you saying to me? I want to be sensitive to the Holy Spirit."*

I thought if he came back by and spoke again, I would witness to him. And here he came. He said, *"Good morning. I hope you have a wonderful day."*

I said, *"Well now, who are you?"* He said, *"I'm manager of the gymnasium."* I asked if I could come visit with him and he said, *"Yes, come in my office at about 11:00."*

I went in and sat across from his desk. This child's heart was breaking over his family divorcing. It was just not a good situation and his heart was broken. He shared some personal things with me and I said, *"Let me just share something with you."*

I shared the gospel with him and across that desk he took my hand and dropped his head on his desk, crying his little heart out. He prayed to receive the Lord into his life.

I went back to my booth and I thanked the Lord that this was a wonderful witness.

"When we find him, we're going to kill him!"

At about 3:00 that evening, I saw this bright light that looked like the sun reflecting on a mirror at the entrance on the other end of the building I was in. Within seconds, standing by my booth looking into the gymnasium where the lights had been turned off, were four teenaged boys. One was popping a bullwhip, one had a metal vest that looked like the hubcap of a car wheel. It was made into a shield and on his back was a pack that had arrows in it and he had on mesh gloves up above his elbows. All of them were dressed in combat fatigues, hats and boots. I heard one of them pop that bullwhip and he said, *"He's not in here, but when I find him I will kill him."*

They wheeled around and took off out the door they had come in where I had seen this light. I realized now that the sun was shining on that hubcap shield. This got my attention and I said, *"God, what are you showing me? What are you saying? What am I to do?"* The Lord said, *"Follow me."*

I looked at the lady next to my booth and I said, *"Would you watch my paintings? I'll be right back."* So I put the camera on my shoulder and I started out that door where they had exited. I had no idea which direction they went. There was an open field and a wooded area to my right, and a residential area to my left. I turned right and those boys were halfway across the field, popping that bullwhip and shaking those arrows.

I had just had knee surgery and had on a skirt. I yelled to the boys and they turned around. I motioned for them to come back and all four of them came. I said, *"I had a booth in the building where you just came in and I overheard you say you were going to kill somebody."*

They said, *"Yes, he wasn't in there. He's probably out here in the woods somewhere. When we find him, we're going to kill him."*

I said, *"Son, I've just had knee surgery and I'm a Southern Baptist preacher's wife and I have something I'd like to share with you. If you're willing to listen, I invite you to sit down on the ground and I'll share it with you."*

I sat down on the ground and all four of those teenagers, ages 14-19 sat down. I questioned them one-on-one, their names, ages and asked them if they had come to the point in their spiritual life that they knew for sure if they were to die today they would go to Heaven. And all four of them said, *"No."*

I said, *"Well, would you like to know for sure that one day you will go to Heaven?"* All four of them said, *"Yes."*

I noticed the tallest boy that had the bullwhip in his hand had on a camouflage cap that had a bill. He pulled it down over his eyes so that he couldn't see me. Well, I caught this but I didn't acknowledge it. I just let God love him right on into the kingdom. As I shared the gospel with them, I noticed the tall one, his name was Tim, begin to roll up his bullwhip up and lay it on the ground. The one that had the arrows in his backpack took them out one at a time and laid those on the ground. They totally disarmed every weapon they were carrying and Tim raised the bill of that cap and looked right in my eye as I shared the gospel with them. They all four prayed to receive the Lord into their lives. I had told them before I witnessed to them that I had had knee surgery and had said, *"I'm going to sit down, but you'll have to help me up."*

I had forgotten I had told them that and when they said amen they were all crying. One of them said, *"Oh, we got to help her up."* They stood me on my feet. I thought I should take their picture so I could remember to pray for them. About that time Tim's mother drove up to pick them up and took the picture with them. This has been 20 years ago. I pray God has called all of them to be special ministers in His kingdom.

As for that bullwhip, the shield and arrows…I learned later that they were all playing the game "Dungeons and Dragons."

-11-

An Empty Mansion

James reminded me this morning as we were drinking coffee on the back porch about another story that took place when I was working in the Burleson Nursing Home. He said, "Nell, there are always other ways to minister other than to lead someone to the Lord and you've been in all those areas. Share another incident."

When I went to work in the nursing home, I was told that we had a resident named Clarence Luttrell who had written 350 gospel songs and they had all been published. One of the songs that he wrote was entitled "An Empty Mansion." Well, this rang a bell with me because when I was 12 years old, I learned that gospel song and I thought, could this be the song that he wrote? So, I began to pray about it.

The next morning when I got to work, I went in his room. Now, I can't recall if he had been in a car wreck, but he had been in a coma for about sixteen months at this time and had not responded to anyone or anything. My job was to motivate the patients' minds. I went in prayed up, and I walked up to his bed. His hands were crossed on his chest under his chin, and they had the covers pulled up to his neck. I just touched the top of the sheet and I said, "Mr. Luttrell, this is Nell Grafton. I'm an activities director here at the nursing home and I love gospel music. I think I know one of your songs. I don't remember all of the words, but the words that I don't remember I'm going to hum." I began to sing, and when I sang that first line he opened his eyes and tears rolled out onto his pillow.

He said, "That's my song. Keep singing." Is that amazing? He came to reality to hear his own music. I went home and got my songbooks out and I found his songs in many of the books that I had. I thank God for this experience.

I went back another day and took a rose. He had his eyes closed, and I put the rose under his nose, not touching his skin at all. I said, "Mr. Luttrell, do you know what this is?"

He said, "It's a rose. Put it over on my TV." It was such a joy to see his reaction and to see him live again. Thank you, Jesus.

-12-

Two Brothers, Heaven or Hell?

I am reminded of this story from a couple of years ago. James and I had been at camp all week with our young people and children. It was a wondrous and glorious time, but we were exhausted when we came home Friday.

I told James that I was going to get up early Monday morning and go to Hampton, AR, to pick blueberries. Come Monday morning, I got up about 6:00 a.m., got to the orchard about 6:30 a.m. I picked blueberries and afterwards, decided to pick some peaches.

I was praying before I ever left, "Lord, just use me for Your glory today." It seems that I was still in the rush that I had been the prior week.

"God slow me down. I am sorry that I have not been your witness. Show me what I can do for you."

As I pulled out of the orchard onto the main road, a cemetery was on the right side of the road. A van was parked in the entrance. A man was standing on the ground by a freshly dug grave. I turned around and went back into the cemetery. As I walked over to where he was standing, I noticed that he was ringing wet from working in the heat. It was exceedingly hot that day. His brother was standing 6 feet into that grave. They had just finished digging a grave for a burial service that afternoon.

I reached out, shook his hand, and told him who I was. I told him that I was just praying that the Lord would show me someone that I could talk to about Him. Then I saw you as I passed by. That is why I came back. I want to talk to you about the Lord. The one standing in the grave was a Christian, and he asked us to include a personal family matter in our prayer.

The one standing up on the ground said, "You know, I never asked Jesus Christ to come into my heart."

"What better time than now," I quickly replied.

The other man crawled out of that grave and held to his brother's hand and mine. There, in a circle, that lost brother was saved. They hugged me, although they were ringing wet, it did not matter. We were praising the Lord for the salvation that God had given that man!

When I am witnessing to someone, I don't try to sum everything up, but after it is over, I realize what God has done. Then I just fall apart and cry and cry.

When I got home, I was just a basket case praising the Lord for what He had done. Then He reminded me of the Scripture, Matthew 24:40 "There shall be two in the field; the one shall be taken and the other left."

Do you realize if Jesus had split those eastern skies wide open before the man had prayed to receive Christ, he would

The Big Pond

have been in Hell and the other would have been in Heaven? Friends, that thought broke my heart!

This is serious to me. This is something I hope I never get used to. I hope I never lose the burden for lost people. I thank God that He gives me the joy of sharing His precious love with lost people.

-13-

Glimpses of Fall

This story concerns cemeteries. When we were in Corning, I got up one morning and told James that I needed to go to Jonesboro, AR that day and do some shopping.

"Pray for me, because I am looking for somebody to witness to along the way."

When I got to Jonesboro I went to Wal-Mart first and as I parked, a 21-year-old A.S.U. student got out of his car also. We had quite a walk to get to the store. I just began to talk with him. I witnessed to him then he took my hand to pray to receive Christ into his life.

He just cried and cried!

"You do not know how I needed this today! I was ready to give up my studies and did not know where to turn. Now, I have a peace and calmness like I have never known before."

I thought this was my witness for the day.

Well, I had to go through Paragould, on my drive home. As I got into Paragould, I was in four lanes of traffic. To my right was a cemetery up on a hill. As far as you could see there were rolling hills and a concrete mausoleum was on top of one hill. I had never seen or been in that cemetery ever in my life. When I had to stop in traffic, I noticed something stir out the right corner of my eye. It was orange, but this was the fall of the year between Halloween and Thanksgiving. Of course, there would be many orange, black, gold, and yellows. Still, when this orange moved, it caught my attention.

"Lord, what are you showing me? What was that?"

"I do not know, but I will follow you."

After going through the next light, I found a little road that was an entrance into that cemetery. I wove my way up to where I thought I had seen that movement. When I got there, I found the grave and flowers that they had placed on the grave, but no one was there. I realized that movement was probably some men that had finished putting the flowers on the grave. Reluctantly, I pulled back on the highway.

"Ah-Ha! I have defeated your witnessing!" Satan said while laughing at my decision to leave the cemetery.

Immediately, God spoke to me as my heart dropped to my toes.

"Follow me," as God picked me up again with a gentle calming voice.

I turned at the next light and went back into the cemetery on a different road. Soon I saw three men standing out in front of the mausoleum. It was about a 4'o clock in the afternoon. I pulled up to their truck. Quickly, I realized that this was a foreman and two inmates that had on the orange vests. They had dug that grave and just finished it.

When I walked over to them, I said, "I know you three men think this is a strange thing to see, a little old woman walking toward you in a cemetery. I saw you here when I passed by and this thought went through my mind, 'what was going through your mind as you looked into the face of death?'"

I told them who I was and what my husband and I were doing in Corning.

The foreman pulled his ball cap down over his eyes in a smirkish manner.

I had seen that before, so I did not acknowledge it.

"I would like to ask all three of you men a question. I ask that you answer me as honestly that you know how, because you can tell me anything and make me believe it and it not be the truth.

However, the Bible says man looks on the outside of our lives. Nevertheless, God knows our heart."

"I will go to Hell, I do not know that I would go to Heaven," answered by all three of them.

As I started to share the plan of salvation, the foreman pulled his ball cap up from over his eyes and said, "Just a minute! Let me ask you a question."

I replied, "Well, fine, I do not know everything, but what I know I will tell you."

"What about the Hindus?"

"Well, what about them?"

"They believe as strongly in their religion as you do in yours. What do you say about that?"

"Well, I do not really know what the Hindus believe, but I believe they worship cows. I have never seen a cow that shed its blood worthy enough to pay for my sins, only Jesus Christ was worthy to do that."

"Oh! Go ahead!" he replied quickly.

I continued with the plan of salvation. In a circle they took my hands and we began to pray.

The foreman says, just another moment, as he reached up, grabbed the bill of his cap, and laid it over on the hood of his truck.

He said, "I am ready!"

I led all three of those men to the Lord.

You know, that was a shaking experience for me! I hugged them all and told them I would be praying for them. Then I gave them all a *New Testament*. I also told the men this was their spiritual birthday. Now they have two birthdays, a biological birthday, and a spiritual birthday. I explained how they needed to get into a church, be baptized, and follow Jesus Christ. As I got back in the car, I was just bubbling over with tears!

When I got home, I went in and James was standing there in the kitchen, and that is when I fell apart. If you had put a windshield wiper on my glasses, it would not have helped, I could not see for the tears.

"James, you are not going to believe what God did today!"

James is so positive. He is my strength.

He was so firm, "Nell, I will believe anything you come in this house and tell me!" Ha! Ha! Ha!

We are very different personalities, I walk by faith and he is an accountant called by God to be His minister. He loves the Lord's work.

I thank God that we have the opportunity to understand how we could work together to save souls going into God's Kingdom.

-14-

Opener or Openee?

When we were in El Dorado, AR, James was pastoring at Parkers Chapel First Baptist Church. A lady in the church asked me if I would go to the jail to visit her son and I told her I would. I really had to pray about this. I was not even sure where the jail was, but one Sunday afternoon I decided this was the time.

I went to the back of city hall thinking the jail would be in the back of that building. I noticed an African-American man at the back door opening the door for families to come in and out that were visiting the people that were in jail. God had it all ready for me to get out. When I got to that backdoor, there was not a person coming out and not one person was coming in. Now this man, a 27-year-old, had on an orange vest.

I was teasing as I said, "Are you the Opener or the Openee?"

"No ma'am, I am a trustee."

Well, this just bolted me right in my tracks! I had not even given a thought that he was an inmate, so I began to witness to him.

Curious, I asked, "Why are you in jail?"

I knew this was not an ethical question to ask — this is what James tells me. Still, you know, God tells me some things to do and I follow His leadership as best I can.

"For selling drugs."

"Well, let me tell you of a better way, there is a better life. Would you like to know about it?"

"Yes ma'am." He had already been sentenced to go to prison.

I shared the gospel with him on the old concrete steps on the back of the city hall. He took my hands and asked the Lord to forgive him of his sins, to come into his life, and to give him the gift of eternal life.

I did not even get to see the other man the lady had asked me to go see, because he was not in that building. This was my appointed witness and I thank God for it. I praised His holy name.

'Naked and you clothed me, I was sick and you visited me I was in prison and you came unto me' (Matthew 25:36)

-15-

The Last Service

When James was in seminary in Ft. Worth I was working for a lady that had a gift shop there in Crowley, Texas where we lived. We had just come back from Montana. The home mission board had appointed us to plant a church that summer of '83 in Ennis, Montana.

This lady came in to the store and I was sharing with her about our trip to Montana and what God had let us do.

She said, "Well, I'm the WMU director at First Baptist Church of Burleson. I would like to ask you if you would go with us women to the chapel at the federal prison the next morning at 6:30 am."

I met with the women, about ten or twelve of us went over to that federal prison that covers hundreds of acres. Now this is a white-collar prison. Most of the inmates are in for embezzlement, drugs, and other white-collar crimes.

When we went into the chapel area there were probably 40 prisoners already gathered in a circle in the room. It was optional that they go to chapel service. The man that played the special music, an African-American, probably in his 60's, had once played saxophone for the Boston Pops Orchestra, a brilliant, brilliant educated man. He belted out 'Amazing Grace' on that saxophone. It was just simply a worship time. I found out later that he had been saved about 2 weeks before we got to the prison and had already enrolled in seminary and was to be paroled in about 2 months. Two of Elvis Presley's bodyguards were also in the chapel during that service. A mother and daughter sat next to me. One of the inmates did the devotional. We sang and were dismissed.

When we got out into the foyer to leave I overheard someone tell the chaplain-who was a very short lady-about a woman who was crying.

"Lord, why did you let me hear this?"

I turned to ask the chaplain if we were allowed to witness in this prison and she said we could. I asked the ladies, "Would all of you wait for me in the foyer, and be praying for me? I'm going back into the chapel room."

When I got back to the chapel everybody had left except one man and one woman. The man had his arm around her shoulder and she was crying her heart out. When I walked up, he just took my arm and put it around her shoulder. Quietly, he walked out of the chapel. She fell over on my shoulder just in tears, "My husband is divorcing me and it's final today."

"Well that's alright."

"I'm losing my home and custody of my children today."

"That's alright. Do you want to come over here and let's talk about it?"

We went over to sit down and she poured her heart out. I shared the gospel with this lady. She was from Helena, AR. I thought this was so ironic since that's near where we came from. I shared the gospel and she prayed to receive the Lord into her life.

I've since learned that because people were bringing drugs into the prison this was the last service that outsiders were allowed to have with inmates inside the prison. But I praised the Lord that this lady was born into God's kingdom that day.

-16-

The Chainsaw Conversion

During 1993-94 James was pastoring at First Baptist Church in Thornton, AR. We were living in the parsonage. One morning I got up and went into the den to sew and as I was sewing I was praying, "God, show me how I could be a witness today. What can I do to glorify You?"

Immediately I heard a chainsaw, but could not detect where the sound was coming from. I got up, went across the hall, and looked out the kitchen window. There is an old house across the street where an African-American man was using a chainsaw to cut the shrubbery, old vines, and trees from around this house. The house was being used for storage.

"Lord, I do not know that man, but I want to be Your witness."

I got a *New Testament* in my hand and started out across the street. I walked up to him and told him who I was. He kindly removed the ball cap he was wearing, and I started to witness to him.

"No, I do not know that I will go to Heaven. I am probably going straight to Hell. I have been an alcoholic, a drug addict, you name it, and I have been there."

Now this man, Clarence, was probably in his early 40's. He was born and raised here in Thornton, so everybody knew him. As I shared the gospel with him, he broke into tears.

"I need God in my life."

I shared the plan of salvation and took his hands as he laid that chainsaw down. Clarence prayed to receive the Lord into his life. I shared this story with some people in the town and in our church.

One year later, I received a phone call and the man said, "Mrs. Nell?"

He told me he was Clarence, then said he was going to be ordained a deacon in the Mt. Zion Baptist Church.

"I wanted you and brother James to be the first to know and am inviting you to the service."

When we got to our church, I told them before a rumor got out that we were going to the black church that night. That is exactly where we would be after our 7:00 p.m. service. We got over to the church. We were going to be incognito and sit on the back pew. That was not to be.

When we walked in the door, they escorted us to the front. Two cane bottom chairs were placed before the Remembrance Table in front of the pulpit. They placed Clarence in one and his wife in the other.

Clarence openly, unrehearsed, told the church that I had led him to the Lord and that he wanted me to stand behind him.

They asked James if he was an ordained man and James replied yes.

They said we would like you up on the platform.

What a beautiful experience this was, how this man is serving the Lord. This was ten years ago, and we still go by his house every day. Clarence is truly a servant of God.

The Big Pond

When I need a lift spiritually, all I have to do is pass by his house and see that wave. That is a beautiful lift for me spiritually, to see the fruits of your work and, seeing God doing beautiful works in people's lives.

-17-

Santa in Heaven

It was Christmas Eve, 1982, and James and I had recently gone through the witnessing program at Immanuel Baptist Church in El Dorado, AR. Our daughter was eight years old and our son was eighteen. About 3:00 p.m. on Christmas Eve, our son asked me to take him out to the mall to finish some shopping.

"Son, that is not on my agenda today."

I had so many things to pull together for Christmas Day, but you know mothers take care of their children.

We got ready and went to the mall. A fountain was in the center of Meadow Park Mall and they had Santa sitting on a platform beside the fountain. Van went one direction and Cristy and I in the other.

After we finished our shopping, we sat across from the fountain. When I looked up, a thought came to my mind . . . witness to Santa. Well, I am not going to make a spectacle out of a witness and I did not want to embarrass anyone so

The Big Pond

I waited until the foyer was clear. No one was coming or going.

I told Cristy to go sit on Santa's lap and talk to him. When you finish, get down, and come back to where we are sitting.

Cristy smiled at me, "Oh, I know what you are going to do, you are just going to witness to him." Your children know you well, so she did just that. I got up from my chair when she returned to our table. The foyer was empty in both directions, so I walked over to Santa.

"Santa? Could I sit on your knee?"

"Yes Ma'am, you can."

This 45-year-old woman sat on Santa's knee. I put my arm around his shoulder.

"Santa, how old are you?"

"I am seventy-nine."

"Do you know for sure that if you were to die today that you would go to Heaven?"

"No." Santa replied.

"Do you want to know for sure that if you were to die today or when you do that you will go to Heaven?"

"Yes Ma'am, what do I do?"

I shared the plan of salvation in a mini capsule. Santa took my hands and as I was holding those black leather gloves, he prayed asking Christ into his life. Children, there is going to be a Santa in Heaven. I praise the name of Jesus Christ, our Lord.

-18-

Sticks in the Sanctuary

Every Christmas, I try to go out of my way to give something that cost me something. Then go to someone that I do not know, and share Jesus and take a gift. When we were in Fort Worth, TX, we were members of Crowley First Baptist Church. Which was a new facility and was probably four years old. They built it in the outskirts of town, in a pasture.

One day at church I overheard someone talking about two young boys that lived in a shanty house right across the road from the church. Obviously, they had not been disciplined, and no had conception how to act at church. I saw one little boy go into the kitchen one Wednesday night and ask for a glass of tea. He simply wanted to take the glass of tea across the road to his mother. They did not have any food.

Then I saw the pastor try to discipline the boy. The other boy had a big stick, and was running in the sanctuary before the service. The boy ducked down with his hands over his head, thinking the pastor was going to hit him. The pastor was simply trying to explain to him that you do not take sticks into the sanctuary.

When I saw this, it simply gave me a burden. I prayed about it and prayed about it and prayed about it.

This was right at Christmas time.

"Lord, I will go to their home. How do I get in?"

I had overheard someone say that her husband, who was not living there at this time, had hired a 'hit man' to kill her. I did not know how to handle this. Without God's strength, I would never have handled this witness.

On Christmas Eve, I told Cristy and James that I was going to get dressed and going to the house to visit this family.

They pleaded, "Do not go."

"I have to, so please pray for me."

Earlier, I had been sitting in the floor picking out pecans — I picked out a pint. I thought this would be an open door for me to take them some food. I put a top on the jar, got in my van and went down to the grocery store and bought a 20lb. sack of grapefruits.

It was extremely cold outside and it had been sleeting. The house was up an incline and my tires slid as I got to the house. When I knocked on the front door, I heard a German Shepherd barking inside.

A woman's voice through the door asked, "Who is it?"

I thought for a moment, well, who is Nell Grafton, I had to give an answer.

"Nell Grafton," I answered.

The woman said, "Well, come to the end of the house and I will let you in."

I slipped on the ice all the way to the end of the house, where the screen was dangling off the porch. As she opened the door, the German Shepherd lunged toward me. She quickly grabbed his collar. "Just a minute, let me put this dog in a room so you can come in."

Just as she grabbed him by the collar, a little white poodle ran between his legs, and stopped at my feet. I reached down and picked up the little dog.
"Oh, I love animals!"
"Well, come on in."
We walked into the kitchen. The only source of heat they had was from a gas cook stove in the kitchen. No boards or doors were on the openings to other rooms. They had hung quilts to keep the heat in that room to stay warm. I sat at the table and she sat on the other chair.
"Well, pull up a couple of more chairs for the boys," I said.
"This is all we have."
"Well, you hold one boy and I will hold the other one."
All I saw was a love for two boys and those boys loving their mother. After sharing the gospel with them, I put the pecans along with the grapefruits in the middle of table. All three of them were crying their little eyes out and prayed to receive the Lord into their lives. I invited the boys to come to children's choir at the church. I told them about the ministerial alliance that had a place in Crowley where she could go to get clothes for the children and for herself.
You know, the next Wednesday night, the mother had dressed the two boys like two Philadelphia lawyers! You know that God is so good. I praise His holy name. He protects me in all situations, as I try to be obedient to be His witness.

-19-

Beautiful Feet

We were living in El Dorado, Arkansas just after James surrendered to the ministry, and we decided to go one Labor Day weekend down to Lake Claiborne and spend the day. We were in his truck, which was a standard shift, and I didn't drive his truck. I didn't even have a key.

So, this beautiful scenic country road up above our place is the road we took into Claiborne that day. We passed an old house place where I had gathered blackberries up in those hills many, many times. There were many African-American people out at the old house place having a family reunion. We got to the trailer, and James was going to go down and work on the pier. It was a very, very hot September day and when he left to go down to the lake, the Lord just spoke to me. In my heart, I could just see all those people at the old house place. I kept wishing someone would come by so they could carry me up there, but then I was reminded that Jesus walked everywhere he went. Who am I? I can too with His strength.

So, I wrote James a note and left it on the kitchen table telling him where I was going. It was probably about a 2-mile walk, so I meandered in and out the little trails up through that hill, and when I got to the house place where they were gathered, I walked in where they were frying fish. Some were out in another area pitching horseshoes, some were riding horses, some playing games, and as I walked in they just welcomed me into that area.

I told them that I was a Southern Baptist preacher's wife, that we had a place down the hill, and that I had something I'd like to share with them and all that would like to hear, I asked to gather around. As they gathered, I questioned all of them as to their names and ages then I asked the question. In that circle every one of them said, "No, I don't know I'll go to Heaven."

Then I asked, "Would you like to know for sure when you put your head on your pillow tonight, that if you were to die or whenever you do, that you would go to Heaven?" and every one of them said, "Yes."

In a circle, they prayed this prayer, "Dear God, have mercy on me, a sinner. Come into my heart and save me from my sin. Thank you, God, for giving me this gift of eternal life. I want to live for you and be your witness. In the name of Jesus Christ, I give you praise. Amen."

I went on to explain baptism, which I do when I witness, explaining that baptism will not save you, but Jesus thought it was very important to be baptized because he asked John the Baptist to baptize Him. It is simply your testimony to the world that when you're put under the water, your old life is passed away and you're coming up out of that water to walk a new life with Jesus Christ. I explained to them that they needed to get into a Bible-believing church and follow Jesus.

When we finished praying, I was just so full of the Lord that I said, "Would somebody in this camp sing 'Amazing Grace'?" Now, let me tell you a lady over next to the fish cooker began to sing and by the time she got to the word "grace," that whole camp had joined in, and they rang the rafters of Heaven as the angels wrote their names down in the Lamb's Book of Life. I praise the Lord that He is so good to let me be in the midst of His working.

When I got ready to leave, I've always been pretty independent, but this was one time I was so dry and thirsty that I had to have something to drink before I made that walk back to the trailer. I asked if I could have a glass of tea. They said they didn't have any tea, but they had some cold canned drinks. I said, "Well, I'll pay you for it" then it dawned on me that I didn't have my purse with me. The only thing I had with me was my camera that was strapped over my shoulder. They gave me a drink and as I turned to leave, I said, "Why don't you let me take a picture of all of you? If you've got a piece of paper, somebody write all of your names down so I can remember to pray for you."

And they wrote their names down on this little piece of paper. Some of them were husband, wife and children in one family and I thanked them and we hugged and embraced and were praising the Lord. I started to leave and they were just waving as I left to go down that hill. When I got back to the trailer, James was sitting at the table. He knew where I'd been and the first thing he said was, "How many, Nell?"

I put the paper on the table and I started counting. There were seventeen people born into God's kingdom that day. You see God gives you the anointing if you have the desire to share the gospel with lost people. The world is full of them. Let's get busy and work in the fields until we see Jesus Christ.

-20-

The Room Next Door

I recall a beautiful experience. In 1993, James was pastoring the First Baptist Church here in Thornton, AR. I was ill and had been taken to the hospital in El Dorado to have colon surgery. I was in the hospital for nine days before I had surgery, then stayed in the hospital another nine days afterwards! Sunday morning after the first nine days, James came back to Thornton to preach for the services that day.

My voice was so weak. I was to the point of a whisper. I picked up my *New Testament* and began to read that morning. Acts 1:8 is just my very favorite Scripture in all of God's Word, because I believe He wrote it for me, and has embedded in my heart.

As I read, "You shall be my witness in Jerusalem." I realized that Jerusalem is right where you are.

"God, I do not know who is in that next room. However, I am going to get my robe on and walk in there to share the gospel."

I shuffled down the hall, knocked on the door and this elderly lady said to come in. I went in and the elderly lady just had major surgery, her daughter was there to take care of her. I told them that I was going to have surgery the next morning and wanted to share something with them. I shared the gospel with them. They said they were lost and did not know if they were going to Heaven, but they do now.

I went back to my room and just began to thank God for His mercy and perfect grace. He is so faithful. If we make one step toward Him, He is always going to lead us through every trial. This will be a victory in His precious, holy name.

-21-

Maid for the Lord

After I had surgery, they moved me to the fourth floor into a private room. I was in the room by myself one morning. My bed, which was by the window, was probably twenty or thirty feet from the doorway to the hall. That morning I began to pray.

"God, I am not going anywhere today, you are so good to me."

Then the door to my room opened and the cleaning lady came in. By her arrogant attitude, I knew she did not want to be there.

"God, help me to witness to her. Help me to touch her, speak to her so that you could touch her."

She was just not happy to be doing the job she was doing that morning.

"Well, do you live here in El Dorado?"

She just made a slur remark, "Well, I am here, but I do not want to be."

"Well, I have something to share with you when you finish, if you would like to listen."

She did not answer me and took the mop, mopped under my bed. Then she cleaned the trashcans, then the bathroom. She cleaned that room, slapping every object around in disgust.

"God, You handle this, please help to love her the way you love me. Help me to portray your perfect love toward her."

When she finished cleaning the room, she wheeled around, started toward the door. When she put her hand on the door, I began to pray.

"God, I have lost her, help me. Please turn her around Lord."

Her hand was on the door handle.

Suddenly, she just made an about-face and came running back over to the bed.

"Did you say you had something to share with me?"

"Yes I do, but you need to get close because I cannot speak above a whisper."

I shared the gospel with this lady.

She broke down and wept. Then, she just crumpled over me onto my chest hugging my neck, and weeping tears that just soaked my gown and pillow. She prayed asking God to come into her life. She hugged me and hugged me.

"Thank you for telling me how I could be saved. You do not know the peace I have in my heart."

"Do not thank me, you thank God, because He sent His son, Jesus Christ, that you might have that gift of eternal life."

That is what life is about for me! I love the Lord and His work. I love people! You know when you are looking at people through the eyes of Jesus Christ. You see souls. You see souls. We have only one life and it will soon be past. Only what is done for Christ is going to last. That is the joy that blesses my soul.

-22-

Musical Elevator Witness

I know the Lord has a sense of humor. I have quite a dry wit too, although I am serious at times. LifeWay in Nashville, TN invited thirty of the Directors of Missions to a conference and the wives could go, if they chose. We were staying downtown in the Sheraton Hotel. Sunday at the conclusion of the conference, they told us that we could go up to the Pinnacle, at the top of the hotel. It was on or about the 28th floor. I forget what floor we were staying on! Everyone was to go to the Pinnacle for dinner at noon.

James always teases me that I trust people not to bother my purse. Occasionally, I will just set it down, sometimes just walk away, go back and get it. Well, this really disturbs him.

We got on the elevator to go up to the Pinnacle after church. When we stepped on the elevator, it was completely glass enclosed. All of the elevators were facing the interior of the hotel.

The Big Pond

Inside was an African-American man standing in a tuxedo, holding a big tub of ice with champagne bottles. He was serving everyone on the elevator. At this time the elevator was full of people.

Sometimes ignorance is bliss and you can get the point across even when it is not proper etiquette or ethical.

After seeing the liquor in the tub, he asked if we would like a drink.

"We are Southern Baptist, and we are teetotalers. We do not believe in drinking anything that has alcohol in it."

Quickly, all eyes and ears perked up in that elevator. This immediately broke the ice, and people were beginning to talk.

"Well, how about some sparkling grape juice?"

"Are you sure it does not have any liquor in it?"

"I am positive."

I told him that we would take one.

He gave James and me a champagne-looking glass then poured the juice in it. When I got off that elevator, I thought that this looked just like everybody else's. People will not know that we are not drinking alcohol.

I told James that I did not feel comfortable with it, and I was putting the glass down. We sat our glasses down and went to eat lunch.

I placed my purse up under the tablecloth of our table. When we started to leave, I forgot it. We returned to the room.

"James, I forgot to get my purse!"

He told me to get on that elevator and go back and get it. Well, when I got on the elevator the same man was serving the liquor. Nobody was in the elevator, but him and me.

"I am a Southern Baptist preacher's wife, and I would like to share something with you. However, I do not want anybody on this elevator to listen except you."

I went to get my purse and returned to the elevator. A couple was on it with me on the elevator and they wanted to go to the second floor.

"Ma'am, what floor do you want to go to?"

I also said the second floor.

He caught the gist of what I had just told him earlier. He let the couple off and that elevator light went on twenty times, I know, on the different floors. When I started talking about the Lord to him, he would pass the floors lit. Then he would go to another floor where it was not blinking. Then he would go down, then up, and back down again. He would go down farther, then he would go back up!

I shared the gospel with this young man.

Quietly, he stopped the elevator, took my hands, and he prayed to receive the Lord into his life. When I got off on my floor, he stepped off and hugged my neck.

"Nobody has ever talked to me the way you talked to me today. I want you to know how much I appreciate it."

I went into my room and got a *New Testament* to give him. This was his spiritual birthday. I filled it out and handed it to him and said there is another note inside that *New Testament* to read later.

I wrote in that note that I would be praying that God would give him a better job so that he would not have to be handling alcohol.

As I was telling James about this later, we got amused.

"Well, this reminded me of musical elevators."

This was a witness where God was the Victor. Praise His name.

-23-

They Could Not Hear Me

Let us go back to Fort Worth, TX, while James was in seminary school. I will share the story of getting this job in another story. I went to work as an activity director in the Burleson Nursing Home. We were living about 5 miles from there.

My coworker's husband was a volunteer at the nursing home. He came there every day. One morning he came in our office and asked, "Nell, every time you come in this building you are as high as a kite! I want to know what makes you tick."

"God, what is Joe asking me? You have to prepare my heart to be able to answer what he is asking."

Joe and his wife were not church people, but they were good moral people.

He said, "I had a dream last night that I was in my casket. I could hear people talking, but they could not hear me."

His wife said, "Joe, just forget it."

"I could not just forget it! Let me talk to Nell." He exclaimed.

I just really went into a deep prayer in my soul. "God, I do not know what to tell Joe. I do not know what he is about to ask, but you prepare me to reach him for you."

"Joe, let us go out into the foyer, and sit," as I touched his arm.

This place was busy, busy with 160 residents, nurses, and nurse's aids. This was a busy place. Suddenly, it was just as though God put an acoustical shield around the two of us as we sat there.

"Joe, did it bother you that you were in your casket?"

He broke and started crying his heart out! He reached into his hip pocket and got a handkerchief. "Yes, Nell, I do not know that I would go to Heaven, as he was wiped tears from his face. Tell me, how I can be saved?"

Then I shared the gospel, right there. Holding to his hands, I led him to Jesus Christ. God gave him that gift of eternal life.

A year or so later, James had graduated from the seminary and we had moved from Burleson. I received word that Joe had passed away. I know where he is today. One day I am going to see him again. He will not have a handkerchief wiping away tears. He will be praising God. Thank you Jesus.

-24-

Sugar or Ceremony?

This is another story that took place when I was working as the activity director in Burleson, TX, at the Burleson Nursing Home. When I first went to work, they told us that a couple of residents were about to celebrate their 65th wedding anniversary. I had taken cake decorating course years before so I knew how to make wedding cakes.

"Well, great let us give them a wedding!"

Everybody that I mentioned this to got so excited. I made a 4-foot tall wedding cake and called Paul Harvey to put it on the news. We also called the *Fort Worth Star Telegram* and they were going to send a reporter out the day of the wedding. We called all the family, the florist, and a jeweler. I called the tuxedo rental store for a wedding dress for her. Everything that I asked for, everyone donated. After calling the rental place to see about renting fixtures to decorate the nursing home for the wedding, they got so excited. They told us to come down to pick out anything we wanted. They would deliver it. We had her wedding dress, his shoes, tuxedo, and a shirt with the ruffles.

The Big Pond

We had the whole nine yards to do a wedding!

Seeing people respond to such a worthy accomplishment was just so beautiful.

"God, I do not know where this couple is spiritually, but I want to know."

One morning, the couple was in the activity room and I told them that I would come to their room about 10:00 a.m. The reporter from the *Fort Worth Star Telegram* would be here at 11:00 a.m. I had a few questions to ask them. I wanted to know how they courted, where they met. Because this was in old, old times, I knew they did not have a car when they were that young. They met me at the door with a tablet an inch thick.

As I sat and began to interview them, she would say, "Let me tell it."

He would say, "No, let me tell it."

Such a precious, precious couple.

I asked how they met and courted back in their younger days.

They began to tell the story.

They said they would go downtown to the courthouse in Bonham, TX and just walk around the courthouse, holding hands. Well, he was probably in his early 20's and she too, when they decided they wanted to get married. Food and other staples were rationed back then because you could not buy sugar or many other items without ration stamps.

Therefore, her mother gave her the stamps one morning and told her to go into town and get some sugar. Well, this is the day they had decided to get married. However, they knew their parents might not approve of it, so they did not tell them. They got downtown and met at the courthouse.

Suddenly, word got out that they were about to go in the courthouse and get married by the judge. By the time they had gotten in to get married, a crowd had gathered and several people were there to witness the wedding. After they got married, he carried her to his home.

They were afraid to go to her home for two weeks. Then they decided they better go home and tell her parents. When they got back home to tell her parents, the news disturbed them.

Well, her dad had a tinsmith shop just across the street from the courthouse. He told her that he had closed the tinsmith shop down when he found out they were married and had left town.

Her mother said, "Why did you not let us know you know that, we would have wanted to be there?"

She said, "All I could think to say was 'Momma, I could not find any sugar!'"

Is that not precious, so precious? We had a good chuckle discussing this and remembering their days from earlier.

The reporter from the *Fort Worth Star Telegram* did a full 2-page article on this couple. I still have the article. It is still precious to me knowing that exactly what they said to him, they had said to me earlier.

"It has just been a joy to work this wedding for you. You deserve it as our gift to you. I just want to ask you a personal question. Have you come to the point in your spiritual life that if you were to die today that you would go to Heaven?"

Now, they were in their 'sunset' years. All they could say about the Lord was, "I love Him, I love Him." They never had a personal experience with the Lord. They had nothing to base their love for Him on and could not discuss their salvation.

I shared the gospel with them. Both of them took my hands and there in that circle of three, God gave them the gift of eternal life.

They are in Glory today because this has been 25-30 years ago.

God is so great and merciful. He just gives us joy to talk about Him every day.

-25-

Eloise's Valentine

This is another special story from the nursing home. We had a woman admitted on my wing named Eloise. She was fifty-six years old. She was not eligible to be in a nursing home. Eloise just had major surgery and sent there for a time of recuperation. I went for the charts so I could fill out her social papers. I saw that she had no church affiliation and began to pray about this. Eloise had personality plus. The residents loved her dearly. She was just an electrifying person to visit with and had one daughter who had small children. I will need to visit with the daughter to fill out all of Eloise's records.

One day her daughter came in.

"Well, let us go out and sit at the table in the lobby so you could help me get this information."

The daughter just dropped her head on the table, as she began to talk.

"I am at my wit's end. My mother is a drug addict and an alcoholic and the doctors would not let me bring her to my home because of the small children. I do not know what I am going to do when the time is up for her to stay in this nursing home."

I began to pray. Eloise had become a special lady to me.

We were preparing to have a Valentine Banquet.

I told the daughter that the residents, not the staff, would choose a king and queen for this banquet. In addition, I believed that Eloise would be chosen. The only clothes that Eloise had with her were the ones she wore to the nursing home after her surgery. I told her that we had a ministerial alliance that supplied clothing for needy families downtown.

I had prayed about Eloise later that night.

The next day I went in her room.

"Eloise, you are a special lady to me and to these residents. I have something I would like to ask you."

"All right."

I witnessed to her as she was lying on her back on her bed. Tears began to flow from her eyes onto her pillow.

"No, I am an alcoholic and a drug addict. I know that if I were to die that I would go to Hell."

I pulled my chair up beside her bed and God just made this witness so perfect. Not one person came in that room while I was witnessing to her.

"Eloise, you are a special person to many people, as I took her hands. You are special to me, but you are also much more special to God."

I shared the gospel with her, and then she prayed to receive the Lord into her life.

"Now, you have the Spirit of the Lord within you. Now you can pray directly to the Father in Heaven, because you are His child now."

I had prayer with her and left.

The Big Pond

A few days later, I had just gotten to work, and sitting in my office with my co-worker. The head nurse came in and said to my co-worker that we were getting Eloise's room ready for her to go into DT's.

She was not talking to me.

She was talking to my coworker.

She said it three times!

"Well, Lord, why am I hearing this? I am not a nurse. I do not know what DT's are. What do I do?"

I turned to the nurse and said, "What is DT's?"

"We are getting Eloise's room ready for her to go into Delirious Trembles. She will be coming off the detox from the alcohol and drugs."

This just made my heart pound.

"God, show me what to do? Show me what to do."

Quietly, I just eased out of the office and to Eloise's room. There was not anyone in her room except her, so I went in. I pulled that chair right back up beside her bed.

"Eloise, Satan's going to come against you! Do you remember when you prayed and asked Christ to come into your life the other day?"

"Yes, I do."

"Then you have the power by the strength and power of the Holy Spirit through Jesus Christ to stand and face anything that Satan throws at you. Do you believe that?"

"Yes, I do!"

I had prayer with Eloise then left out and went back to my office.

She never had one DT!

That is so amazing to me, but it is so real. God is faithful.

He saved her. He delivered her also.

Praise His holy name.

I had the joy of crowning her the sweetheart of the valentine banquet and sharing her conversion experience with her daughter.

That is so wonderful to me. It is so personal that God gave me this. I thank Him that I can share it with others. To encourage people to know that all we have to do is believe and receive.

When we doubt, we do without. We miss the blessings that God has in store for His children and how much He loves us. I praise His holy name.

-26-

Left for Dead

This is another story that is special to me. While I was working as Activity Director at Burleson Nursing Home, my mother and dad lived in northern Louisiana. We had a volunteer that helped me every day with the residents, and her name was Mildred. Her husband was a sheriff in Burleson, TX. He had a ham radio unit in his home.

One morning before I went to work Mom called me. She said an elderly lady out in the country, Mrs. Chester Norris, had been robbed, beaten, tied to the bedpost, and left for dead. The law enforcement from Louisiana was in pursuit of the men that did it, who were heading toward Burleson. Mrs. Norris had gone into town that morning and withdrew quite a sum of money out of the bank. They then robbed her and left her for dead. Mildred came into work and said this story had come over the ham operators unit before she left home to come to work.

"Well, Mom had just called me about this."

The Big Pond

This was so ironic that these two stories would link together, and that I would hear them.

"God, why has this passed my way? Show me what to do."

Shortly after this happened, James graduated from Southwestern Seminary and we moved to Ruston, LA where they called him to pastor a church. I went to a few of the nursing homes to apply for a job as an activity director.

When I got a job at Longleaf Nursing Home, I found out that Mrs. Norris was in this nursing home recuperating. They had a sheriff standing by her door guarding her day and night for fear that whoever had robbed her would return and kill her because she could identify them. This lady had grown up there. Her home was just within five miles of where my husband grew up. This was a heavy burden on me.

"Lord, what if she dies? I do not know where she is spiritually."

I prayed about this, then went into her room. She was black, blue, and bruised all over her fragile body. I sat beside her bed, told her who I was and where I was when I had heard of the incident. That my mother had called to let me know about the incident and that I had been praying for her these months. I shared the gospel with her.

She said she was lost and did not know Christ as her personal Savior.

I presented the plan of salvation to her.

She took my hands. There in that weakened condition, she asked the Lord, Jesus Christ into her life and save her from her sins.

She died a few weeks later, but God had a mansion prepared for her in Heaven. I thank God that He let me put this together just the way He had planned.

Thank you Jesus. I praise your holy name.

-27-

Rose of Sharon

The Lord says, "You shall be my witnesses in Jerusalem, Judea, Samaria, and the uttermost parts of the earth." I have shared all these experiences and now I am going to take you to the uttermost parts of the earth. God has let me go a full circle to fulfill the Scripture, Acts 1:8.

Ten years ago, I had a dream that James and I were getting off a plane in a foreign country. As they were unpacking the luggage, I asked him, "Where are we?" He said, "We are in Brazil." In 2003, ten years after I had the dream, we had the opportunity to go with twenty-four other friends to Sao Paulo, Brazil, to do mission work. I had no clue what I would be doing in Brazil, but I knew I was supposed to go. I did not speak Portuguese.

"Well, how am I going to converse with these people? I like to talk to somebody that understands me."

Well, God had that all worked out too.

When we first got off the bus and went to the first church, people from the church were greeting all twenty-four of us. This lady hugged my neck and said something in Portugese.
"What did she say, Leslie?"
"You look like a beautiful flower." Leslie answered.
Well this really touched my heart. We worked with two Southern Baptist Churches. Mike and Hazel Collins were the resident missionaries. They had the program all worked out when we got there. The women were to teach vacation bible school in the morning at one church.

I led an evangelistic team, and someone else led another team. They gave us an interpreter and a guide from each church. At noon, we would go to another church across town and do the same thing there. I was in my element! This was just what God had prepared me to do.

The first day we went out, my interpreter, Leslie, 17-year-old precious preacher's daughter, was right by my side. She could interpret everything I said and would translate in English what they had said to her. God was in control.

One day, we started down the street from the church.
"Let us go to this house," I told the guide.
When we got there, all of the houses were crude concrete buildings. The buildings were just 6 inches apart and an iron fence guarded every resident. Every one of those homes had a guard dog.

When we got to this particular house, a Doberman Pincer was just inside that gate. The guide would call out to the residents and they would come out. She would tell them what we were about and they invited us either in or not. They invited us into every resident that we went to visit.

When we got to this particular one, this lady in her 40's came to the door. Their dog could have wiped me out with one blow. He was gigantic.

"I will put him in another room," as she got him by the collar. After she put him up, we walked into this 30-40 yard

The Big Pond

portico to her home. A cutting board was probably about 30 yards long next to the wall on my right-hand side. A man was standing behind it.

Well, I have sewn all my life and I love to sew. It was interesting to me to know what he was doing. Patterns lying on top of the fabric covered the entire table. Come to find out, she was a seamstress. The man was cutting out pantsuits and coats, the quality you would buy at Dillard's here in the states. She invited us to come into the kitchen. When you go into their homes, if there are not enough chairs for the family and you, the family will sit on the floor and you would sit in the chairs. She placed a chair for me in front of her. Leslie stood beside me. I started to share the gospel with this precious lady. She was crying her heart out as she prayed to receive the Lord into her life. She got up and hugged us all. She was just jubilant!

The next day we had to walk by her house to go to a resident beyond. Something within me just said go hug her one more time. There was a special bond between that lady and me. As we got to her house, our guide called out, she came and opened the gate. Her teenage son and daughter were there. God had this all worked out, He was way ahead of me, but I wanted to be obedient.

I asked if this man behind the table cutting out the garments was her husband.

She said he was an employee.

I said would you ask him to come over here so that I can share with him too. He came over as I was witnessing to them. She was crying and rejoicing as all three of them prayed to receive the Lord into their lives.

She left the room and went to the inner part of her house. When she came back, she asked me to hold out my arms. Then she put one of the jackets on me and gave me a pantsuit that she had just made. The pantsuit was a little bit small, so I asked her if she could make me one another size. She handed me a stack of fabric samples 4 inches thick and just fanned through them with her finger. "Any color?"

The color rose just kept coming back to me, so I pointed to the rose swatch. Now this was 11:00 a.m. and she said this suit would be made today. God is so merciful that pantsuit is still precious to me, even today.

Awesome! I told her that my husband is preaching at the church up the street tonight and we would love for you to come. She told Leslie that she probably would not be able to come because of her work schedule.

That night as we were at the church, the pastor of the church who was also a lawyer, asked the congregation-about sixty people-to get in a circle. We began to pray for one another and when I looked across the circle, there she stood. Well, I broke the circle. We just met each other in the middle, embracing and hugging each other and praising God! She did get to come to the service.

We went to church that night.

"Leslie, you wrote all the names down? Do you remember the lady that gave me that pantsuit?" She took pictures of everybody that we witnessed to so that we could remember to pray for them.

"Yes."

"Well, what was her name?" I asked.

"Rosa Lee," she said as she handed me a gift of a beautiful flower that the lady had painted in oil for me. I went by the next morning and got the pantsuit.

God is so good. I am so thankful that the painting represented the most beautiful flower of all and that is the Rose of Sharon, who is Jesus Christ my Lord.

-28-

Where is this Child?

James was pastoring at the First Baptist Church of Parkers Chapel near El Dorado, AR. He had bought the book *Doctrine of Prayer* by Dr. Hunt, one of his seminary professors. I was reading his book in the den one morning and it was so deep and meaningful to me.

While reading I began to pray, asking the Lord to show me what I could do for Him today.

Well, I knew about the pond at the Beach Springs Associational Camp. I had fished up there several times before and in my mind I saw a teenage boy about 17-18 years old. He had on khaki cut off shorts and a white T-shirt. I began to pray that God would show me where this boy was so that I could witness to him. I knew in my heart that was what God wanted me to do.

I went to Beach Springs to fish and caught about eleven catfish that I put on the stringer. I always stopped to give the fish to a 77-year-old widow lady there in Smackover. I had

The Big Pond

searched going fishing and returning home so that I could share the gospel with this boy.

It was nearly sundown, so I knew I had to head back home, drive from the pond to the house usually takes me about twenty minutes. As I was going back through Smackover, I stopped and gave the catfish to this lady. She was so proud.

"God, where is this child? It is nearly dark and I have not found him yet."

I turned on a street that I had never been on in Smackover. As I drove one block, there in an open field, was a group of teenage boys and girls playing volleyball. I pulled off the shoulder of the road and got out.

Several of them came to see why I was there. I told them I had something I would like to share with them if they would take time to listen. Then in a circle on that volleyball field, I shared the gospel with seventeen teenage boys and girls. In a circle, they all prayed to receive the Lord into their lives.

When I opened my eyes from praying for them, there was that boy straight across the circle from me. He had those khaki shorts on with that white T-shirt. Tears quickly welled up in my soul and I walked over to him.

"Son, what is your name?"

"Adrian."

"I am going to be praying especially for You, I pray God will call you out to be His minister."

God is so good. I hope I never get used to seeing people born into God's Kingdom. If they have soul, God gave them that soul and they have the right to the Throne of Grace, just like we do. Oh, help us to be faithful just to talk about Jesus.

-29-

Seven Teens

This is another story while James was pastoring First Baptist Church at Parkers Chapel. We moved into a new home. I taught the College and Career class in our den Sunday mornings before we built the church. Across the street was a family that later became members of the church and they had a son named Jamie. I went over to their house and invited Jamie to attend, and he did.

One day, I shared the gospel with the entire group. I questioned them one on one, their age, name, and had they come to a point in their spiritual life that they knew for sure that if they were to die today they would go to Heaven. Every one of them gave the perfect answer to this question.

Two weeks later, I was sick in bed with the flu. I heard someone knock on the door and our daughter went to answer it.

I heard her say, "My mom has the flu."

The Big Pond

With this firm persistent voice, I heard someone say, "Get her up, I need to talk to her!"

I got up, put my robe on, and walked in the living room to see this young man, Jamie.

He hugged me, cried, and cried.

"Mrs. Nell, remember that question you asked two weeks ago in Sunday School?"

"Yes, I do."

"I lied. I have been miserable ever since."

After calling James into the living room, we shared the gospel with this young man. Jamie prayed to receive the Lord into his life.

A few days later, Jamie and his dad had been down on the Ouachita River fishing at Lock 8.

Jamie knew how much James and I loved to fish, but since James could not take the time off this day, Jamie asked his mom if he could take me down to catch some of those bream. I asked James and he said, "I do not see why not."

Jamie and I talked about what we were going to do with the fish we caught. I knew that we did not care anything about eating bream.

"Well, let us just pray about it. We will use these fish as a tool to be God's witnesses. We will give them away and we will witness to them."

This is exactly what God had planned.

Although it was a beautifully clear, sunny day, a small cloud hovered in the sky, but did not look too threatening. We went out in the river about 300 yards from the landing. Between the landing and us were some 100-foot tall cypress trees.

We had caught about thirty-five huge bream in a very short time.

Suddenly, a bolt of lightening came out of that one cloud and hit one of those cypress trees. The tree split and burned to the root in the deep water. After the limbs came back up to the surface, they floated on the water like toothpicks.

The Big Pond

This was so sudden, I did not say a word. I just pointed toward the landing.

Jamie cranked that boat motor up and we headed to the bank.

We began to look for someone to give our fish to. We had gone about three blocks through the neighborhood when we saw seven older teenagers coming toward us.

Jamie stopped, rolled the window down asked if they would like to have the fish. They were excited to have them, so we followed them to their house to get a pan to put them in.

We shared the gospel with seven lost children, spiritually. They all prayed to receive the Lord into their life.

You see, God gives us every opportunity and we miss so many. He gives us a blessing and joy of sharing with those that we are faithful to share.

Several years later after we moved up to Corning area, Jamie's mother called us. She wanted to let us know that her husband had surrendered to the ministry and so had Jamie. They are preaching the gospel today. That is God and I praise His holy name.

-30-

Bride of Christ

We lived in Thornton, which is about 7 miles away from Bearden. Our daughter, Cristy, had graduated from high school in Bearden, AR. We moved from here and were gone to Corning, about seven years and moved back here to Thornton.

Cristy had recently gone through the faith seminar and loved to be God's witness too.

One day, when Cristy and I were in Fordyce we parked next to a car in which there were two boys. Cristy realized that they had graduated with her from high school and they recognized each other.

I looked at Cristy with a gleam in my eye.

Both were dressed in white tuxedos and they were about to be in a wedding at 2:00 p.m. (it was about 1:00 p.m. now).

I shared the gospel with them. They were lost spiritually. In a circle of four, they prayed to receive the Lord into their life.

You see. They were groomsmen wearing white tuxedos.

God also made their hearts clean, fresh, and anew. They became a part of the Bride of Christ that day. Praise the name of the Lord.

-31-

2 Vans

I have to share this story about our son, Van. The sponsoring church that we were associated with, in Ennis, Montana, was Kirkwood Baptist Church in Bozeman, Montana. The pastor and his wife called after we returned to Fort Worth, TX for seminary. They asked if Van could come up there and go to college and stay with them. He was nineteen at the time.

After about two weeks, Van called on a Sunday night. He told us that at church that night he had asked Jesus Christ to come into his heart and life and forgive his sins.

What a testimony! The Lord cleansed his soul.

The next morning I went to work. Alice, the lady that I worked with knew that I loved to pick up pecans and said, "Nell, I want to take you down to a little town park where there were many pecan trees."

It was so very cold outside.

"I do not really want to get out in this cold weather."

"Well, you have to see these trees. They are just loaded with pecans."

I began to pray about this. We put several *New Testament*s in the car in case we could find someone to witness to. Alice was a beautiful Christian. We went to the park.

While looking at the trees we noticed a man about 400 yards away, by a small stream there in the park.

"Let us go witness to him."

"Wait, I need to pray about this before I get out."

I got a *New Testament*, put it under my jacket and we got out to walk over to him. He was a retired civil service worker, about 65-66 years old. His wife had just passed away. He was standing there by that riverbank grieving his heart out, crying.

"Talk to him Nell."

I shared with him how the Lord had prepared for those that trust and believe in Him and confess Him as Lord and Savior.

"Is this what you wish to do so that you will know one day you will go to Heaven?"

"Yes, I do!"

He was crying uncontrollably, he turned around and took our hands.

I led him in the Sinner's Prayer.

This was my first witness since the night Van had called that he had been saved.

Guess what this man's name was? Van.

This is so precious to me. Seeing God work throughout the world with His children is awesome to me. I thank Him that He gives us the opportunity, the joy and privilege of simply calling on the name of Jesus.

-32-

Delton

My mother had a brother, Delton, who had been in the Navy. He married a Filipino lady. He had retired and was living in the Philippines. Later he developed cancer because he was exposed to asbestos on some military ships back during the war. Delton loved my mother and dad. When he was on furlough, he would always go to their house, so I did not realize how terminal he was. After his diagnosis, he later moved to Kodiak, Alaska. My mother and her sister flew there to see him.

We had just accepted the mission work in Waxahachie, TX to be sponsored through First Baptist Church of Waxahachie. We were going to be working in a mobile home park where there were 1,200 people. We were packed and ready to put the boxes on the van. Then the Lord put Delton, my uncle, in my heart. I did not know how terminal he was, I just knew he was sick. I called my mother and asked for his telephone number. She said he probably could not talk you.

I called and he could only speak with labored breathing. He answered the phone.

"Delton, this is Nell. I want you to know that I have been praying for you, Mom and Dad love you so dearly and I care where you are spiritually. Could I ask you a question?"

He said, "Yes."

I asked him that if he knew for sure that if he were to die today, that he would go to Heaven.

"No."

Well, it took about two minutes, a mini gospel, but it was full of truth and saving power. Delton prayed the prayer and asked Jesus Christ to come into his heart and life. He is in Heaven today. I thank God that my mom and dad are with him.

It will be a great homecoming one day when we see Jesus face-to-face. Then we will sing that sweet story, 'Saved by Grace.'

-33-

My Last Breath

~~~

*L*et us go back to the big pond in Thornton! One day, I began to pray, "Lord, if somebody is at that big pond I will be your witness." The levee covers the length on one side of the pond, which is 21 acres. I went in on the lower end of the pond to start fishing. I had put three fish stringers in my tackle box. The fish just happened to be biting that day. I put three or four bass on the first stringer and put those over in the water. They weighed around 2-2 ½ pounds each. I kept working myself to the other end.

I saw a lady fishing on the other end of the pond. After I got about halfway up, I had about 3-4 more bass to put on a stringer. The fish were all about the same size.

I kept working myself closer to her, by now I had three stringers in the water. She saw me catch all those fish. Obviously, that caused conversation.

"Have you ever fished a bass tournament?" she asked.

"No, I am waiting for Hank Parker to call, so I could fish in a tournament with him."

Noticing that she had a 5-gallon bucket, "Well, what have you caught?" I asked.

It was summer time and very hot. In that bucket she had caught probably a half-bucket full of 2-3 inch bream. The fish sat in that heat.

"You need to put some water on these fish or they are going to ruin."

"Oh well, I cannot swim. I am deathly afraid of water," she replied in a sad tone.

"Well, let me have the bucket. I will put some water in it for you."

I went down the bank and filled the bucket with water as best I could.

"Would you teach me how to bass fish, I do not know how?"

"Why, of course."

So I sat on the bank, opened my tackle box and had her bring her line over. I sat there on the bank and rigged her rod and reel up for bass. I showed her how to catch one.

Well, before she threw it back in, I witnessed to her. She prayed to receive the Lord into her life.

She said, "You know? I now know why I was spared. My husband and I went fishing a few weeks ago. I had a dream the night before that someone was drowning. I cannot swim and we were out fishing. I asked my husband to put me out in the boat. He was going to sit on the bank. He just gave me the paddle and let me go over to a little area to fish. The next thing I knew, I was at the bottom of the lake. I knew I was breathing my last breath because I cannot swim. My husband got me out of the lake and saved my life. Before I had that dream, little did I know that I was going to be the one that was drowning. Now I know why God spared me. I had a sister that I have cared for all her life. She died the night before September 11, 2001. God spared me to raise that child and come to the point today that I could come to Jesus in saving faith."

God is so good. We had prayer. It was a jubilant time for both of us!

She took that rod and reel, with a plastic worm that I had put on it, threw it out and on the first cast, she caught a 3½ lb. bass. The fish was bigger than any that I had on the three stringers!

"My husband is not going to believe this," as she reeled the fish to the bank.

I went back down the levee and got all my stringers. I emptied those fish into her 5-gallon bucket.

It was a joy to share, not only the fish, but also Jesus, which was the most rewarding experience for that day. You see God gives us those fish. We can give a man a fish and feed him for a day, but we can teach him how to fish and he can fish for a lifetime.

About the Authors

Nell Grafton

*E*arly on in her teen years Nell Grafton felt the call of the Lord in her life to be his witness.

She and her husband, James, were each born and raised in the tiny sawmill town of Dubach, Louisiana, which is in the piney words of North Louisiana. They were friends, then high school sweethearts and finally were married in September of 1955. At the time of this printing Nell and James will have just celebrated their 50th wedding anniversary!

Nell had longed to be equipped to witness. When she was 45 years old, her pastor brought a witnessing program called 'Evangelism Explosion' to their church. Nell, James and a few others trained for three months. In turn they each trained two people over the course of the next three years. At this time Nell and James both knew the perfect will for their lives was to "pick up their cross daily and follow Him!" And they still do that to this day.

Nell's simple motive for sharing these stories is to let people know that anyone can answer the Lord's call on their life. In her own words, "Just be sensitive and committed and go!"

"I cannot help but speak of the things I have seen and heard!"
(Acts 4:20)

If you'd like to have Nell speak at your special event please call (870) 352-3398

Matt Mosler

Matt Mosler (www.mattmosler.com) is a writer, speaker, singer and former television and radio personality. He worked as a meteorologist and talk show host for television stations in Alabama, Mississippi, Texas and Arkansas before God yanked him out of his boat and into full-time Christian ministry.

Matt is the founder and director of Beautiful Feet, Inc., a ministry intended to inspire, encourage and motivate Christians to step out of their boats, fulfill their ministries and become the person God created them to be. He speaks more than 150 times a year for schools, churches and corporations.

Matt is married to Camille and they have three children, Travis, Madison and Rebecca. They make their home in Sherwood, AR.

This is his first book.

(Very special thanks to Peggy Green McIntosh and Cathy Penny Hill for their assistance in editing this project -MM)

If you'd like to have Matt speak at your special event contact him at matt@mattmosler.com